P9-DDF-745

SHELTER dogs

SHELTER dogs

traer scott

MERRELL
LONDON · NEW YORK

For my dad, who gave me so many opportunities; my mom, who passed to me her immense love of animals; my husband, Jesse, for being the best human being I have ever known; and for all of the beautiful dogs in this book who were not fortunate enough to find a loving home.

ACKNOWLEDGMENTS
Many thanks to the organizations and individuals who helped to make this book possible: Providence Animal Control; Out of the Pits; Amy Sirenski, the most devoted volunteer I have ever known; Dina Supple, Tyler Lewis, Shana Cobin, and all of the dedicated folks at the Providence Animal Rescue League; Stephanie Georgia.

A portion of the proceeds from sales of this book will be donated to animal welfare and rescue causes.

First published 2006 by Merrell Publishers Limited

Head office:
81 Southwark Street
London SE1 0HX

New York office:
49 West 24th Street, 8th Floor
New York, NY 10010

merrellpublishers.com

Publisher: Hugh Merrell
Editorial Director: Julian Honer
US Director: Joan Brookbank
Sales and Marketing Manager: Kim Cope
Associate Manager, US Sales and Marketing:
   Elizabeth Choi
Managing Editor: Anthea Snow
Project Editors: Claire Chandler, Rosanna Fairhead
Editor: Helen Miles
Art Director: Nicola Bailey
Designer: Paul Shinn
Production Manager: Michelle Draycott
Production Controller: Sadie Butler

Photographs copyright © 2006 Traer Scott
Text copyright © 2006 Traer Scott
Design and layout copyright © 2006 Merrell
   Publishers Limited

All rights reserved. No part of this publication may be reproduced, stored in a retrieval system, or transmitted, in any form or by any means, electronic, mechanical, photocopying, recording, or otherwise, without the prior permission in writing from the publisher.

British Library Cataloging-in-Publication Data:
Scott, Traer
Shelter Dogs
1.Dogs – Pictorial works 2.Dog rescue –
   Pictorial works
I.Title
636.7'00222

ISBN-10: 1 85894 352 3
ISBN-13: 978 1 85894 352 7

Designed by 3+Co.
Copy-edited by Kirsty Seymour-Ure
Printed and bound in China

Jacket, front: Petey
Jacket, back (clockwise, from top left): Abby, Terrier,
   Riley, Austin, King, Minpin
Page 2: Dumbledore
Page 5: Adonis
Page 14: Puppy
For information on all these dogs, see pages 90–94.

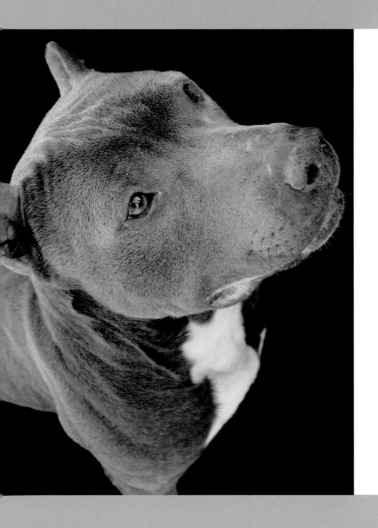

Introduction

This is a series of portraits that resulted from frustration, opportunity, and loss. I have always been fanatical about animals. As a child, I never had dolls—only stuffed dogs, cats, horses, and perhaps the obligatory bear. My first entrepreneurial venture was a neighborhood dog-sitting business at the age of seven. At eight, my stamp collection boasted colorful canine stamps from all over the world. I trick-or-treated for the SPCA instead of Unicef and wrote odes to my cocker spaniel. As an only child in a single-parent home, I spent much of my childhood and adolescence alone, save for my dogs. I had friends, but always felt that my animals were more compatible company. In junior high I began picketing fur and animal testing, circulated petitions, and stopped buying leather. In college I was "that PETA [People for the Ethical Treatment of Animals] girl who picks up strays"; at that time, in agriculturally driven North Carolina, "vegetarian" was almost a dirty word. I have always extolled the many virtues of mixed-breed dogs, urging friends and neighbors to adopt from local animal shelters rather than buying from breeders. Yet, in all those many years of advocacy, fund-raising, and dog obsession, the one thing I never did was actually *volunteer* at a shelter. I tried, but every time I walked in, tears would come to my eyes the second I made eye contact with one desperate face. Everyone agreed that I just didn't have the constitution for it. My friends suggested that I could continue to do good in other ways, but I always felt disappointed in myself.

One Christmas a few years back, my husband, Jesse, and I were in charge of organizing a holiday staff party. We encouraged the guests to bring gifts (toys, food, and blankets) for homeless animals, which were to be donated to local animal shelters. I was to play Santa and deliver the goods. One stop I made was to a Rhode Island city shelter. After unloading my boxes of donations, I forced myself to walk through the rows of kennels, wide-eyed and deafened by the plaintive barking of more than twenty dogs.

*Opposite: A husky casts a furtive stare
in my direction as I snap his photo.*

Above left: Bailee jumps
at the cage, pleading to
be taken outside.
Above right: Potential
adopters tour the kennels
at the Providence Animal
Rescue League.
Opposite: A newly adopted
male is sedated before being
neutered. Many shelters
require dogs to be altered
before they are allowed to
leave with their new families.

I kept being drawn back to a sweet little female pit bull in one of the last cages. When I inquired about her, I was told that she, along with the male beside her, was to be "put down" in a day or two. Their time was up, and no one had shown interest in them. The next day, I coerced a friend down to the shelter, and we adopted both dogs. Jesse and I kept the male, and our friend kept the little female. We thought she was still pudgy from puppyhood, but actually she was pregnant. She delivered nine healthy puppies. We adopted the scrawny runt of her litter, which gave us a total of three dogs in our urban third-story apartment. My husband made me promise to stay away from animal shelters.

The following year, I began photographing and writing, *pro bono*, for a new regional monthly called *The Animal Print*. One of my first assignments was to interview Katenna Jones, a Brown University graduate student and the director of Brown's Canine Behavior Program, which had been funded by a private grant. The aim of the program was to teach volunteers how to train dogs who were in animal shelters, and determine whether such training affected the adoption and retention rate of those animals. Ms. Jones and her student participants found that there was a strong trend indicating that animals who were trained and socialized and who received regular exercise were adopted more quickly and retained longer in their new homes than animals who received no interaction or training.

After writing the piece, I suddenly felt very tied to the program. I decided to volunteer under Ms. Jones's watch. It was only one hour a week at first, and I took comfort in her strength and dedication. She was empathetic when I became emotional, but she always directed me back to the work. Jones gave every dog a name, taught them new tricks as well as trust, knew their habits and preferences, and then pleaded for their lives to be spared when all of the kennels became full. The first time that a dog I had been working with was euthanized, it was devastating. Unfortunately, it is an inevitability that I have now had to face dozens of times. Like most shelter workers, I have found a private way to mourn.

All of the animals we worked with had been abandoned or lost by their owners. They were rarely neutered or even wearing identification. Very few were ever reunited with their owners. Some dogs had been beaten or severely neglected. Others had been handed over simply because

it was no longer convenient for their owners to keep them. Ms. Jones taught us to do temperament evaluations, to estimate age, and to teach basic obedience. Most dogs love to learn, to have a "job," and I am always amazed at how proud dogs seem after learning a new trick.

Eventually, Ms. Jones's grant ran out, and she accepted a full-time position at a different shelter, where she could continue her work. Her student volunteers either graduated or moved on, leaving me and one or two other people. I felt I had no choice but to stay. As a photographer, I was soon asked to begin taking photos of all the dogs for records and for internet adoption sites. As my files grew, I realized that many of the dogs whose pictures I had in my archives never made it out alive. Despite our efforts, many dogs had to be euthanized simply to make room for the dozens more brought in every week by Animal Control. I found that no matter what, I couldn't bring myself to delete their photographs, which in some cases were the only record of their existence. A few months later, I decided to begin creating true portraits of these dogs.

From day one I conceived of this project's becoming a book, a body of work that would help document and memorialize some of the beautiful, intelligent animals I meet in shelters. A group of fifty or so would represent the millions who die each year in animal shelters nationwide. I was never interested in making images of desperate dogs behind bars. While photographs of that nature are valid as a means of illuminating the situation, I feel they evoke little more than pity in the viewer. I wanted to strip away every environmental element and create dignified individual portraits that presented each dog's unique personality. By singling them out and temporarily raising them above their statistical status, the issue is made much more personal. When people view these images, they are often locking eyes with a captivating being who has been cast aside, abused, or left behind.

To me, these are portraits in the simplest and truest form. I had to do very little. My subjects were already beautiful, animated, and ready for their close-ups.

I used only natural light and an Olympus digital camera with a surprisingly sharp macro lens. When time and situation would allow, I set up backdrops. The rest of the time, I removed the background debris in Photoshop. Beyond simple lightening, darkening, and basic clean-up, there are no significant digital alterations to any of these images. I usually worked with a volunteer assistant and a large box of dog treats. It would take anywhere from five minutes to more than an hour to get the "right" shot of each dog.

Every dog reacts differently to a camera. Some immediately perceive it as the voyeuristic device that it is, and refuse to look at the photographer. They will literally duck, hide, or turn in circles to avoid having the camera meet their eyes. Other dogs interpret the camera as a direct threat. Watching through the lens as a dog lunges straight at one's face is a very humbling yet cinematic experience. After a few years of this, I have now trained myself to click the shutter when it happens. So far no real damage has been done to me or my cameras. Other dogs are not patient enough to wait for the treat I am offering in exchange for a few still moments. While trying to stay in a sit, they start squealing and wriggling their bodies, barely able to stay attached to the ground. If I take too long, I get a big sloppy tongue planted on my lens. Then there are what I like to call

the "Oracles." As soon as a camera is pointed at these dogs, they just fix their gaze on you and pour out volumes. They seem to be telling a story that is much longer and more epic than the one their short lives can feasibly encompass. The Oracles (very often pit bulls) seem to transform from jumpy and slobbering to prophetic and back again all in the short time it takes to snap a few photographs.

In this work I have made a point of trying accurately to represent all the diverse breeds and ages of dogs who pass through U.S. shelters. There are purebreds, almost indeterminable mutts, five-week-old puppies, fourteen-year-olds with rotten teeth, and of course pit bulls. Many of the dogs in this book are pit bulls or pit mixes, which is an important and accurate repre sentation of the situation in many urban shelters. Every day, as I walked down through the kennels, there was one pit after another. Nine out of ten are sweet, playful, loyal dogs, but no one wants to adopt them. According to ASPCA research, a third of shelters surveyed do not adopt out pit bulls, either because it is against the law to have them in their communities, or out of concern that the dogs will end up in abusive situations. The modern plight of this breed is tragic.

Unfortunately, most people know the pit bull only by its sensationalized media reputation, which is biased and reactionary at best. I have worked with countless pits; I also have one sleeping under the covers with me every night, and I can say without hesitation that they are my favorite breed. They are incredibly intelligent, affectionate, tenacious, playful creatures. I have been bitten by a dog only twice in my work at shelters—once by a poodle and once by a Chihuahua. During

Above, from left to right: Most dogs try desperately to catch the attention of anyone walking by the kennels. A woman surrenders a litter of puppies to a city pound. Many shelters participate in humane education programs, such as the Providence Animal Rescue League's Pets and People exhibit at a local children's museum. A pit bull puppy is surrendered with other litter mates to a city pound.

the past two years, I have bathed, brushed, temperament-tested, wrestled with, and taught dozens of pit bulls, some of whom had been badly abused or neglected. None has ever so much as bared its teeth at me, despite being scared and displaced.

Opposite: Although his fluffy friend was adopted within days. Tiger (on the left) waited six months for a home. In this photo. the pair look forward to a few of the treats that are often handed out by visitors.

Life at a shelter can be a psychologically devastating experience for a dog, even if it eventually gets adopted to a good home. Dogs are caged and surrounded night and day by the deafening barking of other frightened animals. Most shelters that I have visited (especially city pounds) share common woes. They are understaffed, underfunded, and overcrowded. Some dogs are let outside their kennels only once or twice a week. They try desperately to catch the attention of anyone who walks by. Many become distraught and panicky, constantly pacing, chewing, and clawing at the cage. Some even begin harming themselves. What they want more than anything is attention from people. They want to play ball and have their backs scratched and be outside in the sun. What often makes the difference to an animal's coping ability—and therefore its ultimate fate—are the volunteers who take it out, play with it, give it bones to chew on, or simply teach it to "sit."

I wish I could count how many times someone has said to me, "I don't know how you do this. I could never handle it." The truth is that no one can handle it. After more than two years of relentless experiences in shelters, I still come out and cry. Then I go back in and meet a new dog who needs our help, and it starts all over again. Psychological defense mechanisms are a mixed blessing. They allow me and every other shelter worker to keep doing our work, but in the process, names and dates and fates are often forgotten. Yet no one ever forgets a face.

What amazed me most when I began to look back at this series was the intense emotion, dignity, and even humor that I saw in each face, despite the circumstances in which the dog was forced to live. Every photograph was taken while the dog was housed in an animal shelter. Some found good homes; others, less lucky, were euthanized.

SHELTER dogs

Diamond

Sage

Austin was a typical beagle—
strong-willed, scent-obsessed,
and very talkative. This shot was
taken between loud outbursts
of passionate baying.

Austin

Shadow

Barry

Bailee

Puggle

Rosie

Bonnie

*Bonnie beat a lot of odds.
She survived the trauma and
aftermath of Hurricane Katrina.
Moreover, she was one of a very small
number of pit bulls who were
fortunate enough to be rescued and
rehabilitated after the disaster.*

Bunker

Tiger

Captain

Timmy

Celeste was a frenetically hyper dog who never stopped moving. I have always found it odd that this was the one good shot I got of her. My camera captured a fleeting moment of repose that lasted less than five seconds.

Celeste

Shady

Stanley

Copper

Dumbledore

Minpin

Smokey

Swinger

*Abby broke my heart. She had
a painfully sweet disposition
and fierce intelligence, but
no one wanted to adopt a dog
with so many undefined health
problems. She seemed to know her
fate from the very beginning.*

Abby

Rosie

Malaki

Spanky

Frankie

Hercules was a quintessential mutt with a hero's name. Yet when I first viewed my images of him, I was truly shocked. He managed to project an astounding sense of majesty and breeding. When I look at this photo, I am reminded of the beauty and nobility that lurk inside even the most common-looking canine.

Hercules

Jack

Yogi

Jake

Fluffy

Joshua

King was a goofy, happy puppy whose tongue could never keep up with the rest of him.

King

Winston

Stubbs

Sadie

Minerva

Nellie

Springer

Molly

Nicoh

Poppie

Puppy

Fenster

Oliver

Bear

Ox

*Ox was the class clown.
His comical mug matched
his charming personality,
and he was always ready
to show off to his fans.*

Sophia

Pandora

Petey

Riley

Terrier

Who's who

These notes reflect the condition of each dog on its arrival at the shelter. Many shelters require animals to be spayed or neutered before going to a new home.

Abby, page 47. Seven-year-old unaltered female shepherd mix, picked up as a stray. Abby was terrified when she came to the shelter. Her body was riddled with tumors, and it was clear that she had been used to birth numerous litters. Abby was one of the sweetest dogs I've ever met. She was playful and energetic and displayed no symptoms of illness, but the tumors made her unadoptable. She was euthanized in December 2005.

Adonis, page 19. Two-year-old neutered male pit bull, picked up as a stray. Like many dogs, Adonis was shy when he first came in. After a few days of adjustment, his true personality began to show. Adonis was transferred after one month to the New York Animal Farm Foundation, where he earned his Canine Good Citizenship and became a certified therapy dog. He was still up for adoption at the time of writing.

Austin, page 20. Three-year-old un-neutered male beagle, picked up as a stray. Austin was a typical beagle—very talkative, bright, and stubborn. Like most small dogs, he did not stay at the shelter long; he was adopted after seven days.

Bailee, page 25. Eighteen-month-old spayed female pit bull/Great Dane mix, picked up as a stray. Bailee was depressed while at the shelter and lost weight rapidly. Her owner claimed her after a few weeks, but in a month she was back, having got loose again. Her owner was unable to get breed-specific insurance and turned her over to the city. Bailee was euthanized in February 2006 because the shelter was overcrowded.

Barry, page 23. Two-year-old un-neutered male standard poodle, turned in by his owners because they had too many animals. Barry was an eager, friendly dog in desperate need of a haircut when he came to the shelter. Two weeks and one grooming later, he was adopted.

Bear, page 81. Four-year-old un-neutered male Rottweiler, picked up as a stray. Bear was very friendly and playful while at the shelter. He was adopted after twenty-two days.

Bonnie, page 29. Two-year-old female pit bull, rescued from New Orleans after Hurricane Katrina in August 2005. Bonnie was taken to New York by volunteers from Out of the Pits. After her photo was posted on the internet, the shelter was contacted by people claiming to be her owners. She remained in foster care until a positive identification was made, and was finally reunited with her family in April 2006.

Bunker, page 30. Two-year-old male pit bull, rescued from the New Orleans area after Hurricane Katrina. He got his name because he dug a bunker for himself at the Tylertown Rescue Facility to stay cool. Bunker's quiet manner and charm made him a favorite among his rescuers in New Orleans. He was taken to Out of the Pits shelter in upstate New York, along with other Katrina pit bulls. Bunker was adopted after three months.

Captain, page 33. Five-month-old un-neutered male Border collie mix, turned over by his owner, who was deployed by the military. Captain was very hyper and loud at first. Consequently, he didn't get adopted as quickly as most puppies, but he found a new home after thirteen days.

Celeste, page 36. Two-year-old unaltered female purebred Siberian husky, picked up as a stray. She was adopted after three weeks.

 *Cocker*, *page* 35. One-year-old un-neutered male purebred cocker spaniel, picked up as a stray. He was adopted after five days.

 *Fluffy*, *page* 59. Four-year-old male Eskimo spitz, surrendered by his owners because he kept escaping. Fluffy was adopted out twice and both times returned for biting. He was euthanized in February 2006.

 *Copper*, *page* 41. Eighteen-month-old un-neutered male yellow Labrador retriever, turned in by his owners, who were moving. Copper was a handsome, energetic young Lab. He was adopted after nine days.

 *Frankie*, *page* 53. Two-year-old un-neutered male American pit bull terrier, picked up as a stray. Frankie was one of the volunteers' all-time favorite dogs on account of his intelligence, amazing temperament, and playful, loving personality. After months at the shelter, however, he began going kennel-crazy. He was taken in by the Animal Farm Foundation in March 2005 and rehabilitated, and was then adopted after two months.

 *Diamond*, *page* 17. One-year-old unaltered female American pit bull terrier, picked up as a stray. Diamond was a very happy, playful dog even while at the shelter. Her owner claimed her, then turned her over to the city. She was adopted after a month and a half.

 *Hercules*, *page* 54. Six-year-old un-neutered male shepherd mix. Hercules was abandoned by his owner in a house. He was a very intelligent, energetic, loving animal, with the enthusiasm of a much younger dog. He was still available for adoption after a month and a half.

 *Dumbledore*, *page* 40. Eight-year-old un-neutered male shepherd mix, picked up as a stray. Dumbledore's sagelike graying face and doleful eyes prompted his name, after the headmaster in the *Harry Potter* series of books. He was amazingly energetic and sweet. Dumbledore was transferred to a private shelter and was finally adopted after one month.

 *Jack*, *page* 56. Two-year-old un-neutered male brindle Labrador/collie mix, turned in by his owner, who was moving. Jack was adopted after two weeks.

 *Emma*, *page* 49. Two-year-old spayed female pit bull mix, picked up as a stray. Emma was emaciated, terrified, and riddled with worms when she first came in. Now she is a playful, talkative girl who loves playing with tennis balls and other toys. She was adopted by a police officer after two and a half months.

 Jake, *page* 58. One-year-old male Doberman mix, turned in by his owners because his barking disturbed their neighbors. Handsome Jake was a very bright, affectionate young dog with boundless energy. He was adopted after one month.

 Fenster, *page* 78. One-year-old un-neutered male Chihuahua/wire-haired dachshund mix, picked up as a stray. Fenster was found as a feral living in a city park with a pack of other small dogs. After three weeks at the shelter, he proved very friendly. He was adopted after one month.

 Joshua, *page* 60. Five-year-old un-neutered male shepherd mix, picked up as a stray. Joshua was quite hyper and weighed in at around 85 lb. (39 kg), making him unappealing to most urban adopters. He was transferred to a more rural regional shelter, where they had the space and time to work with him. He was adopted after two months.

King, *page 62*. Eight-month-old un-neutered male Siberian husky, turned in by his owner because he "tore up the house." King was full of energy but very eager to please and to learn. When he saw someone approaching his kennel, he would sit quietly and wait. He was adopted out once and immediately returned because he wasn't good off leash. He was adopted for keeps after one month.

Nellie, *page 70*. Six-month-old unaltered female Labrador/pit bull mix, picked up as a stray. She was adopted after two weeks.

Lhasa, *page 65*. Three-year-old female Lhasa apso, picked up as a stray. She was adopted after one week.

Nicoh, *page 75*. One-year-old un-neutered male Akita/Siberian husky mix, turned in by his owners, who were moving. Nicoh weighed in at around 70 lb. (32 kg) and was a bundle of energy and enthusiasm. He was adopted after eight days and now lives with three other rescued dogs.

Malaki, *page 51*. Two-year-old un-neutered male pit bull mix, picked up as a stray. While moving to Florida, Malaki's owner left him in the care of a friend. Malaki got out and was picked up on the street by Animal Control. When the owner was contacted, he decided not to claim his dog. Malaki was euthanized in April 2005.

Oliver, *page 80*. Two-year-old un-neutered male American bulldog, picked up as a stray. Oliver was very friendly to people but severely aggressive toward other dogs. He was euthanized in January 2006.

Minerva, *page 68*. Three-year-old female poodle mix, picked up as a stray. She was adopted after five days.

Ox, *page 83*. Three-year-old un-neutered male American bulldog, picked up as a stray. Ox was 90 lb. (41 kg) of charm and drool. He was adopted after two weeks.

Minpin, *page 43*. Two-year-old un-neutered male miniature pinscher mix, picked up as a stray. He was adopted after one week.

Pandora, *page 84*. One-year-old unaltered female pit bull/Catahoula leopard dog mix, picked up as a stray. Despite Pandora's exceptional beauty and sweet temperament, she was very slow to find a home on account of her hyper, puppy-like behavior. Weighing around 55 lb. (25 kg), she jumped on everyone, even toddlers, and scared away many potential adopters. She was finally adopted after three months.

Molly, *page 73*. Two-year-old unaltered female pit bull. She was adopted after one month.

Petey, *page 87*. Eight-month-old un-neutered male pit bull, picked up as a stray. Petey's owner was contacted but never came to get him. Petey was a sweet, playful puppy with a plaintive stare that won everyone over, but his log number (666) actually drove away superstitious potential adopters. He was adopted after five weeks.

Poppie, *page 76*. Two-month-old male pit bull puppy, picked up as a stray. He was adopted after one week.

 *Sadie*, *page 69*. Five-month-old female pit bull mix puppy. Sadie was relinquished by her owners because she was "too hyper with the new baby." She was adopted after two weeks.

 *Puggle*, *page 26*. Three-year-old female pug/poodle mix. She was transferred to a less crowded rural shelter after five days, from where she was adopted.

 *Sage*, *page 18*. Four-year-old female pit bull, turned in along with the other family dog (Smokey) because her owners were moving. She was adopted after a month and a half.

 Puppy, *page 77*. Eight-week-old pit bull mix puppy. This puppy's mother was picked up by Animal Control when the pups were five days old. The owner of the dogs had no license or insurance (needed because of breed). The puppies were confiscated and brought to the shelter to be with their mother until insurance was obtained. Their owner never came back. The mother dog was euthanized. All the puppies were adopted.

 *Shadow*, *page 22*. One-year-old unaltered female pit bull, picked up as a stray. After being claimed by her owner, Shadow was back at the shelter four days later. Outside, she was cautious but friendly and engaging. In her cage, however, she was severely depressed and very dog-aggressive. Shadow was euthanized in November 2005.

 *Riley*, *page 86*. Three-year-old un-neutered male Rhodesian Ridgeback mix, picked up as a stray. Because of his friendly, playful personality and expressive face, Riley was one of my personal favorites. After a long stay at the shelter, he was adopted by an inexperienced first-time dog owner. Three days later, she brought him back, claiming he had tried to attack her. Riley was euthanized in April 2005.

 *Shady*, *page 39*. Five-year-old female pit bull mix, turned in by her owners because they were moving. Shady was affectionate, playful, and, best of all, seemed to flash a nervous, toothy smile when she was excited. She was adopted after two and a half months.

 *Rosie*, *page 27*. Three-year-old female Chihuahua, taken from a domestic abuse situation. She was adopted after twenty days.

 *Smokey*, *page 44*. Ten-year-old female Border collie mix, turned in (with Sage) by her owners, who were moving. Smokey was found to have arthritis and was put on medication. During her spaying, the vet discovered that she had bladder stones. Despite her condition, Smokey was adopted after a month and a half. Her adopters have since called to thank the shelter for giving them such a great dog.

 *Rosie*, *page 48*. Two-year-old unaltered female boxer, abandoned in an apartment. Rosie was intelligent, engaging, and full of energy. She was adopted after two weeks by a motorcycle aficionado, and now rides on his bike, sporting her own helmet.

 Sophia, *page 85*. Five-year old pregnant female shepherd mix, picked up as a stray. Petite Sophia was covered with a skin infection and was petrified when she was brought in. She had a shy, sweet, and very loyal disposition. Sophia was transferred to another shelter, where she gave birth to five healthy puppies. She and her litter were then taken into foster care. She was adopted by a nursing home after her puppies were weaned.

 **Spanky**, *page* 52. One-year-old un-neutered male pit bull, picked up as a stray. Spanky's intelligence, exuberance, and mild temperament with both people and animals made him a true ambassador for his breed. He spent four months at the shelter and then another eight months in foster care before finally being adopted.

 **Springer**, *page* 72. Five-year-old male springer spaniel, picked up as a stray. He was adopted after one week.

 **Stanley**, *page* 38. Seven-year-old un-neutered male collie mix, picked up as a stray. Stanley was very gregarious, barking his thoughts and concerns to us constantly. He was adopted after two weeks.

 **Stubbs**, *page* 66. Two-year-old male Australian shepherd mix, picked up as a stray. Stubbs was so named by a volunteer on account of his stubby, docked tail, which he wagged constantly. He was reunited with his owner after two weeks.

 **Swinger**, *page* 45. Three-year-old male pit bull, rescued in the aftermath of Hurricane Katrina. Swinger was transferred from New Orleans to Out of the Pits shelter in New York. He was soon taken into foster care by a shelter volunteer, who ended up adopting him.

 Terrier, *page* 88. Three-year-old un-neutered male terrier mix, picked up as a stray. This little guy didn't even stay at the shelter long enough to receive a name; he was adopted after five days.

 Tiger, *page* 31. Seven-year-old un-neutered male pit bull, relinquished because his owner's child didn't like him. Tiger was a trooper, waiting patiently in his cage for someone to come and play with him. Stubborn but intensely lovable, he was finally adopted after six months.

 **Timmy**, *page* 34. Eight-month-old male pit bull, rescued from New Orleans in the aftermath of Hurricane Katrina. When the levee broke, Timmy's owner was not allowed back in to get her dog. She had been looking for him for weeks when she happened upon his photo on the internet, with a link to Out of the Pits shelter in New York. Timmy (real name Dema) was reunited with his family two months after the hurricane.

 **Winston**, *page* 64. Four-year-old un-neutered male Siberian husky/American bulldog mix, picked up as a stray. Winston was very friendly and enthusiastic, but his size (about 80 lb./36 kg) was a deterrent to adopters. He was adopted after seven weeks.

 Yogi, *page* 57. One-year-old un-neutered male shepherd mix, picked up as a stray. Yogi was a very energetic, playful dog with a charming, expressive face. He broke our hearts when he failed his temperament evaluation. He was euthanized in June 2005.

Sources and resources

Facts and figures

The following estimates are provided by the Humane Society of the United States:

- Between six and eight million dogs and cats enter shelters each year.
- Between three and four million dogs and cats are adopted from shelters each year.
- Between three and four million dogs and cats are euthanized by shelters each year.
- There are between 4000 and 6000 shelters in the United States.
- Only an estimated 30% of dogs entering shelters are ever claimed by their owners.
- 25% of dogs in shelters are purebred.
- A fertile dog can produce an average of two litters each year, with each litter averaging six to ten puppies.
- In six years, one female dog and her offspring can theoretically produce 67,000 dogs.
- According to the *Journal of the American Veterinary Medical Association*, the most common reasons why owners hand their dogs in to animal shelters are:

    no obedience training;
    lack of veterinary care;
    dogs being sexually intact;
    dogs having daily or weekly housetraining "accidents."

What you can do

- Adopt an animal from a shelter, and encourage your friends and family to do the same.
- Make sure your pet is microchipped and/or always wearing identification.
- Before getting a dog, do your homework: Research breeds, visit shelters, and find the right dog. A dog is forever.
- Donate your time or money to shelters, animal welfare groups, or spay/neuter programs.
- Above all, SPAY or NEUTER your dog, and encourage others to do the same.

Charitable organizations

UNITED STATES

The American Society for the Prevention of Cruelty to Animals (ASPCA)
aspca.org
The largest, most powerful, and best-respected animal welfare group in the country, the ASPCA is a major force in the shelter world. Although it actively educates and advocates for all animal welfare issues, dog and cat overpopulation is its main focus.

The Humane Society of the United States (HSUS)
hsus.org
HSUS initiatives cover a broader spectrum of issues than those of the ASPCA and have a stronger activist tone. Humane Society International (HSI) has expanded the activities of the HSUS into Central and South America and across other continents.

Best Friends Animal Society
bestfriends.org
Best Friends helps individuals, humane groups, and entire communities across the country set up spay/neuter, shelter, foster, and adoption programs. It was also instrumental in rescuing many of the thousands of animals left homeless by Hurricane Katrina in 2005.

North Shore Animal League America (NSALA)
nsalamerica.org
NSALA is the world's largest no-kill animal rescue and adoption center. The league rescues, nurtures, and restores pets to happy and healthy lives in loving homes across the country. To date, it has rescued almost one million dogs, cats, puppies, and kittens.

Animal Farm Foundation
animalfarmfoundation.org
This rescue organization takes in pit bulls, spays or neuters them, and provides obedience training before placing them in new homes.

Out of the Pits
outofthepits.org
Out of the Pits is a nonprofit pit bull rescue group that places an emphasis on public education.

Pit Bull Rescue Central
pbrc.net
Pit Bull Rescue Central is the definitive national pit bull education and rescue organization. Its website has a searchable database.

INTERNATIONAL

International Fund for Animal Welfare (IFAW)
ifaw.org
IFAW is a broad-spectrum animal welfare organization that is active in dozens of campaigns. Its mission is to "engage communities, government leaders, and like-minded organizations around the world and achieve lasting solutions to pressing animal welfare and conservation challenges."

AUSTRALIA

RSPCA Australia
rspca.org.au
RSPCA Australia is a national organization that campaigns on a variety of animal welfare issues. RSPCA shelters around the country care for more than 130,000 animals each year.

Humane Society International Australia
hsi.org.au
Established in 1994 as a branch of Humane Society International (see HSUS above), HSI Australia is committed to relieving animal suffering and preventing animal cruelty in Australia and the Pacific Rim.

CANADA

Canadian Federation of Humane Societies (CFHS)
cfhs.ca
Initially founded to help local humane groups across Canada lobby for better protection of farm animals, CFHS today serves as the national voice for a variety of animal welfare issues.

Humane Society of Canada (HSC)
humanesociety.com
HSC campaigns on a wide range of animal welfare issues. Its website includes details of lost and found pets, and animals needing a new home.

UNITED KINGDOM

The Royal Society for the Prevention of Cruelty to Animals (RSPCA)
rspca.org.uk
A committed shelter/adoption advocate, the RSPCA investigates and prosecutes animal cruelty cases, educates, and supports all animal welfare issues.

Dogs Trust
dogstrust.org.uk
The largest dog welfare charity in the United Kingdom, the Dogs Trust runs rehoming centers around the country. Its mission is to work toward the day "when all dogs can enjoy a happy life, free from the threat of unnecessary destruction."

Battersea Dogs & Cats Home
dogshome.org
Battersea, in south London, is the largest and most famous animal shelter in the United Kingdom. It rehomes up to 5000 dogs and 3000 cats each year.

The Mayhew Animal Home
mayhewanimalhome.org
Mayhew is one of the busiest animal shelters in London. It rehomes thousands of abused, neglected, or abandoned animals—dogs, cats, and rabbits—each year.

Last Chance Animal Rescue
lastchanceanimalrescue.co.uk
Last Chance is a major rescue center for dogs, cats, and other small animals, based near Edenbridge, Kent. It operates a nondestruction policy.

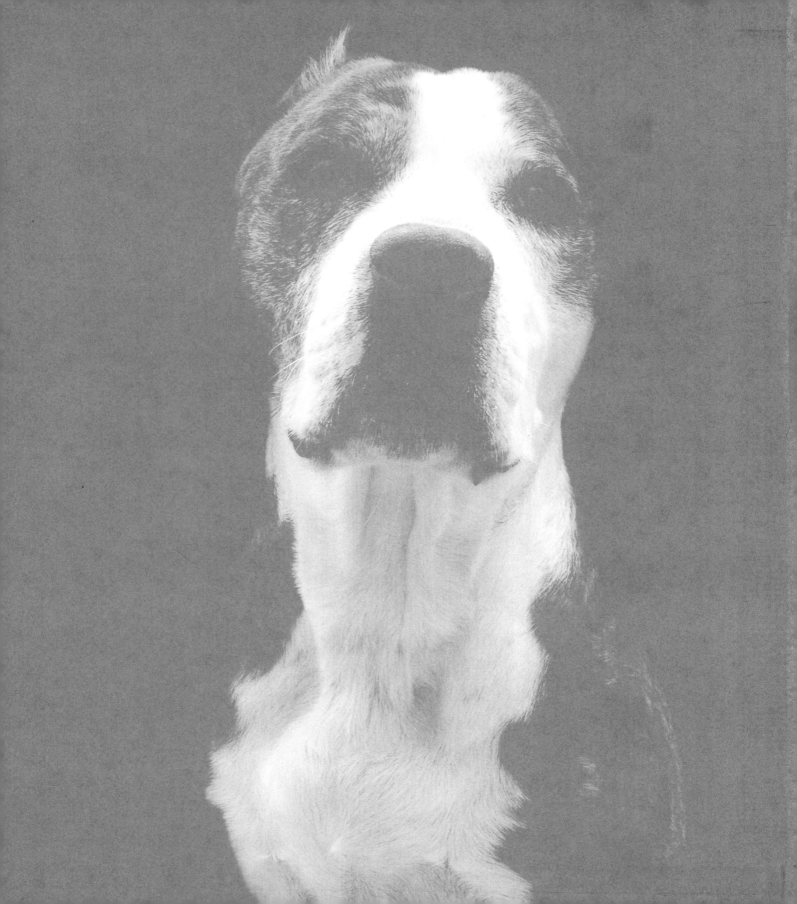